GW00993613

The Beginners Guide to Facebook Marketing

Table of Contents

Introduction

So, you're one of those zillion people out there who are looking to make it *virtually* big in a world that is very *real* out there? A world where there is a fine line between the *virtual* and *real*? Well, you're not alone. In today's world it is hard to ignore the customer who finds the product or service you are trying to sell online; in fact, a majority of customers are going the virtual route in order to glean which product or service will best fit their requirements as well as budget.

This shouldn't really come as a surprise, because there is undoubtedly a treasure trove of information online and that's the very first place people are going to look, especially when they are looking to compare their choice of product with others in the market, before going in for the final purchase. Of course this is where you want to step in and ensure that *your* product gets their eyeballs rolling like no other and that it is the one selected over several others, simply on account of some rather stellar Facebook Marketing.

In this book you will learn all about what it takes to create a successful Facebook Marketing campaign. You will see that it is really rather easy to get the kind of visibility that you could otherwise only have dreamed of, by following some really simple strategies that have been especially selected from a vast multitude of tactics, in order to give you only the best possible outcome where it comes to making that Facebook Marketing campaign of yours most successful.

So, it's time to delve deeper into the process of Facebook marketing in order to discover just how we can captivate the minds of the hordes of people who scour the Internet daily, in order to convert them into happy customers of ours.

Chapter 1: The Why of Facebook Marketing

Before we dive deeper into the essentials of Facebook Marketing, it's important to take a good look at just why Facebook Marketing is the #1 social media marketing platform of choice, where it comes to promoting your product.

The importance of Facebook marketing

 # It has the largest number of users

Facebook has by far the largest number of global users as compared to any other social media platform out there, as well as the largest number of American users. So, whether you're looking to go global or perhaps even limit your marketing to within the country, you will find that you're most certainly using the social media-marketing platform of choice.

It's less formal than other platforms

You will find that it is most easy to strike a conversation with people on Facebook than it is on a platform like say, Twitter. The very essence of Facebook is casual and the people using it will be more than happy to get into a conversation with you when it comes to that product or service you are trying to sell.

Facebook has the highest conversion rates

Where it comes to the conversion rates among all the social media platforms out there, Facebook has the highest. Of course you want to target those customers who are already using similar products out there in a big way; those are the very customers who will be prone to using your product time and time again!

 # You can easily find the business contacts that matter to you

Not only does Facebook have the highest number of users as we have already discussed, but it also has almost every single person you know, using it. Remember the time you connected with that classmate of yours – the classmate you had last met twenty-five years ago in high school? Well, you can as easily find the business contact you just met for coffee twenty-five *minutes* ago, on the very same platform! Yes, it gives you the chance to instantly reach out to people who are intrinsically connected with your business, and helps you literally *break the ice* with them – the act of connecting with them on Facebook is completely different than connecting with them on a *serious* platform like LinkedIn, after all.

It drives the largest share of social media referral traffic

Where it comes to social media referrals, Facebook is the ultimate king over other sites like Twitter and YouTube, and it is most certainly a great idea to indulge in Facebook Marketing for this very reason. After all, there's nothing quite like a referral where it comes to that product of yours getting the attention it deserves – that only goes to show people out there that your product is tried and tested by others who are happy using it. That most certainly helps your product score brownie points over the competition!

You reach a vast amount of customers out there – for practically free!

This reason's pretty obvious, but one must understand that even though Facebook is free, its impact on building your brand must not be taken in the slightest. In fact, you will be spending only a fraction of what you would be spending on regular channels of marketing like print and television ads where it comes to the Facebook marketing campaign that we will discuss in far greater detail over the course of the subsequent chapters, but the reach and effect of your campaign is phenomenal, that too with the least possible costs involved!

It helps in relationship building over time

Last but not the least, it's a great way to connect with your business associates, clients and customers. You will find that in today's world a vast majority of interaction is virtual, and connecting via Facebook is simply a great way in strengthening that relationship you have established with them and taking it to new heights, thus benefiting your business in a most remarkable fashion. It's not merely about retweeting someone's tweet and then forgetting about them for long; it's about actually forming meaningful connections that will be sustained well over time...

Chapter 2: The 7 Facebook Marketing Campaign essentials

Now that we have seen just how absolutely essential Facebook marketing is where it comes to promoting that product of ours, let's take a look at how we can effectively champion that Facebook marketing campaign, to ensure that our product is taken to greater heights. The absolute first thing that is required is an understanding of the Facebook marketing campaign essentials, without which all our marketing efforts will go to waste.

The 7 essentials of a Facebook Marketing Campaign

 # Understand exactly what your mission is before you create that Facebook page for your business

Sure you might be selling a great product, but what is it about your product that makes it ever so interesting? What is it about the product you offer, that will make people out there want to choose it over others? What exactly is it you are trying to sell? Think long and hard over these questions and it will help you better craft that Facebook page of yours, keeping in mind the unique brilliance of your product.

Set very clear goals

The only way to get somewhere in that marketing campaign of yours is to actually establish where that *somewhere* is, in the very first place. You will come to see that if you set some very clear-cut goals where it comes to that Facebook strategy (like attaining 1000 likes in the next three months), then you will have a sense of direction and purpose and will pull all stops to ensure that you do at least come close to those 1000 likes (if not supersede it by a large margin)!

Take a good hard look at your Facebook page before you start marketing it

The first thing you need to do before you go all out marketing that Facebook page of yours, is to take a good and hard look at it to ascertain whether you are really providing something of value to that end customer out there. You have to ask questions like, 'Is it exciting?' and 'Will it pique the curiosity of the person who has landed here to discover more about my product?' True, you have to first work on that page and make it as captivating as it can possibly be, before working on that marketing campaign. That will make all the difference between getting 10 likes and *100 likes*, when you do set it out there for one and all to see!

Have a stellar company website

Of course that Facebook page of yours is going to be used to lure customers out there to come and visit your company website. That is where they will come to see exactly how professional your company is, and learn more about your product as well. You might even want to have those ecommerce capabilities built into that website of yours so that customers can buy your product if they are interested. The last thing you want is for one of the links on your website to be not working, or copy that is written rather shoddily. You have spent a good deal of time and effort in crafting that Facebook page of yours, right? Well then make sure that you pay a good deal of attention where it comes to working on that website of yours as well, or else you will find that all your marketing efforts where it comes to that Facebook page of yours, would have gone down the drain!

Research your audience well

It is absolutely imperative that you spend a good deal of time doing some rather astute research where it comes to that audience of yours, because otherwise you will not be getting the right results out of your marketing campaign. You can see the pages that your already existing clients frequent and get a better idea as to what their tastes are and how you can get even more potential customers in the process. For instance, if you're in the meat business the last thing you want to do is target people who are looking for vegan organic food! Make sure that you have the right target audience in mind, before going all out with that marketing campaign of yours!

 # Have a tracking plan in place where it comes to those goals of yours and learn to be flexible

You have set a goal for yourself as discussed in the second point in this chapter where it comes to your Facebook marketing, right? Well, the last thing you need is to discover that at the end of one month you have only 300 likes, as opposed to the 1000 that you so earnestly wanted. The only way you can ensure that you actually get somewhere is to have a tracking system well in place. So, you could perhaps monitor your progress every week or so to see how the strategies you are implementing (the ones that we will be discussing in the next chapter) are working. If things are not quite going the way you want them to, you will come to see that you can perhaps reframe that marketing campaign of yours and work more on a particular strategy that seems to be working more than others out there. The important thing to bear in mind here is to be flexible – that is a sure shot recipe for success!

Use Google Analytics to track those conversions

You might have ten thousand likes on your page, but what's the use if only a small percentage of the people who have liked your page, has bought your product? Using Google Analytics you can actually track how many customers have actually bought your product, and that is when you will discover just how effective that campaign of yours really is. When you are setting your goals, make sure you include this number as well. It might not be as many as those likes, but it's far more important as far as the bigger picture is concerned!

Chapter 3: The Top 10 Facebook Marketing Strategies

So, we've successfully gone into all that we need to bear in mind well before we actually take the plunge and implement that vital marketing campaign that will help our brand get all the recognition it deserves in the marketplace out there, right? Well, it's time then to take a look at the top marketing strategies that will actually help leverage our brand to those dizzying heights!

The top Facebook Marketing Strategies for unparalleled performance of your brand

 # Find out the best times to post

Of course you're going to be posting a lot of content, but do you even know that it is absolutely vital to ensure that your post is actually *seen* by that target audience of yours? Sure you might have a lot of fans, but you're really not achieving anything if you post at erroneous times when most of your fans are not online.

If you post in the times they are offline, then the chances that your page will get lost amongst the hundreds of others that make it onto the news feeds of your clients, is pretty high.

The best way to overcome a problem like this is to use the *Insights* feature on your Facebook page. This will help you determine the average time when that fan base of yours is online. In that way you will almost certainly ensure that they don't miss out on what you're trying to tell them every single time you post that great content of yours!

Give your fans some incentives

Your fans are only going to be your fans if you keep things exciting for them for long enough, and one of the surefire ways to do that is to offer them some tangible incentives, albeit those which will come to them with a clause.

For instance, if they get their friends to sign up for your email newsletter, they could be rewarded with freebies or perhaps discounts on your products in the time to come.

In that way it will be mutually beneficial for the both of you and you will find your business growing by leaps and bounds simply because people like things that are free. Of course you might wish to limit the number of freebies (you could give them away when they get ten subscribers for you instead of lesser – in which cases the discounts would be their incentive).

Use video content

Although you shouldn't be posting videos all the time, using them can be a great way of captivating the minds of people browsing through your Facebook page, and it is certainly one of the better methods to generate interest in your product. The beautiful thing about video is, you can use it to tell a story in the most unique manner possible.

Of late, there has been a great spike in the number of people who are turning towards video to get all the information they need. You could get some to make a professional video for your brand or you could simply do it all by yourself. Just be sure that you don't make the same kind of videos all over again.

You should leave the audience guessing all the time as to what you are going to come up with where it comes to that video, so that the experience is always refreshing and delightful for them. You will also find that there are greater chances that videos will appear on your users' timelines, rather than mere status updates.

Send out that email newsletter

Now that you are on Facebook, it's really important that everyone should know about it, and more so the people who have a real interest in what you are trying to say. These are the people who have signed up for that email newsletter of yours, and it would be a tragedy if they were to be completely oblivious of the fact that your product is on Facebook.

So, you need to ensure that you send out that email newsletter to everyone that is on it, stating that you are indeed on Facebook and that this is the place where you will find all the snazziest updates where it comes to your brand. In this way you will get an almost instant following from a lot of people, simply because they are the most likely people out there to click on that *Like* button on your Facebook page.

The best time to send out those emails is in the mornings. Of course, you want to do this on weekdays as well, preferably on Mondays. So, set those email marketing tools like *MailChimp* to work and make that campaign of yours even more effective!

Give your page that personal touch

The last thing you want, really, is to make people out there believe that you are constantly trying to sell them something (even though, inadvertently, you really are). So, instead of simply harping on about your product, you should add a bit of flair to that Facebook page of yours and infuse it with some really exciting content.

One of the most effective ways to do this is to post something really inspirational every now and then. You could even post a picture of the glorious sunset taken from your company meeting, or perhaps even the cake that you cut for one of the founders' birthdays. Do anything that you can to make it a bit more personal. The very fact that your page is on Facebook, implies that you are in a far more personal environment as such, and being as friendly as you can with your audience will only make your Facebook page all the more endearing to them.

Besides, your page will not come across as something that is merely mechanized, but rather as a *living entity* that is there to ensure that you always stay inspired and happy!

Create those status updates of yours on a regular basis

Of course you will not be posting videos all the time; for the better part you will have to rely on those status updates to catch the attention of people out there. One of the things that you have to bear in mind is this: if you really want to be popular on Facebook then you have to ensure that you post on a regular basis.

One of the best ways to ensure that you do so is to schedule those status updates of yours to be posted at a future date. By doing so you will not only ensure that you don't miss out on posting when the opportune time comes, but also that any great idea that you might have stumbled upon at any given moment is not lost over the course of time.

Research has shown that when you use emoticons in your posts there will be a far greater chance that they will be liked and shared, than if you don't. It will also ensure that you get more comments on them, and that is important because it gives you a great chance to interact with your audience!

Ask questions to boost interaction

One of the best possible ways to interact with that audience of yours on Facebook is to ask plenty of questions. You will see that when you do this, there is a greater chance for interaction than when you don't.

It also gives people out there the feeling that you truly care about their needs and more importantly, value their opinion.

Once they get this sense of being valued, they are more than eager to answer whatever question you might have posed on that page of yours. The best part is, when they actually answer your question it gives you an opportunity to interact with them in a way like no other. For instance, you might be asking them about what they feel about the proposed color of your product that is going to be launched soon.

They might come up with a reason why they feel another color will be more suitable. That might just spark off a conversation between you and them in which you might even possibly learn a thing or two.

Besides, it will only show the person who has posted that comment (and all the other people reading that thread) that you do genuinely care about your audience!

Use Facebook Ads

Using Facebook ads is a really great way to ensure that you take that Facebook Marketing of yours to another level altogether. You will find that they are really not all that expensive.

Forget the thought of even comparing the cost of Facebook advertising to the costs of traditional advertising – you're really paying virtually nothing at all and at the same time reaching a large audience out there.

There are different kinds of ads that you could choose from, ranging from ads to simply increase the likes on your Facebook page in order to create a larger fan base, to ads that will encourage people to install an app that you might have designed especially for your product.

Make sure to use the ad that you feel is most appropriate for your business. As discussed earlier, you want to use the Google Analytics tool to target the right audience.

Also, the best possible way to make that ad of yours stand out amongst so many others is to use a captivating picture and a rather stellar ad description to go with the same.

Use photos along with those status updates and for your profile

Every now and then it might be a really good idea to post a picture along with that status update of yours. It is well documented that a post with a picture receives more likes and shares than one that does not. When you're posting a picture, it might not be a bad idea at all to post one that has been professionally shot (as we have discussed in the case of videos).

Besides, it's really hard to miss a status update that has a picture in it, simply because it takes up a lot of space. One of the best things about posting pictures is that they allow you to tell stories, even if they are not as visual as their *video* counterparts.

Make sure that you also include a cover photo for your Facebook page.

That is the thing that will really stand out when someone visits your page, and you want to make sure it absolutely encapsulates the very essence of your company.

That being said, you want a great profile picture for your Facebook page as well. A well-taken photograph can serve to be much better in this instance than merely something you have found off the Internet.

 # Promote your page well by using contests to your advantage

One of the best possible strategies you could use, where it comes to effectively promoting your page out there, is to use Facebook contests that will serve only to your advantage simply because the lure of a contest is far too great for many out there to resist.

Of course there will be something in it for the person participating in the contest, and you have to make sure that you give them something that is appreciated, like perhaps the very product you are trying to sell or another related freebie that will be most appreciated by them.

The kinds of contests you can run can vary; you could even do something as simple as putting up a picture and asking your target audience to come up with a caption for the same.

Of course you want to promote that contest of yours as hard as you possibly can, so that you reach the maximum number of people possible. The fact is, contests are most engaging and fun and will help you retain your existing fans as well as help you get a whole lot more!

Chapter 4: The Top 10 Facebook Marketing Tips

Whilst we might have procured all that valuable information in the earlier chapter where it comes to making the most of that Facebook Marketing of ours by using only the best possible strategies possible, let's take a look at the top Facebook Marketing tips that we can incorporate into that marketing campaign of ours, in order to make it even more effective than it already is.

The top 10 Facebook Marketing tips to take your brand to greater horizons

 # Tip 1 – Join Facebook marketing groups

Of course one of the best ways to get experience is to learn from others out there who might be in your industry; all you have to do is follow certain Facebook marketing groups that allude to your industry and you will see that you are able to uncover a whole treasure trove of information where it comes to marketing your brand.

You will come to see real life examples of people who have tried several marketing methods that you might be on the verge of employing, in a bid to ascertain whether they might really be the strategies that you should go in for. While you might wish to only join those groups that pertain to your industry, it might not be a bad idea to join general business groups as well – so that you have an idea of the right kind of direction your business should be taking!

Tip 2 – Lure those people out there with fan-only content

You need to make the people who have liked your page feel special if you want them to go so far as to actually buy your product or service, and one of the best possible ways you could do that is by providing them content that only they have access to, on account of their having liked that business page of yours.

This does not mean that others out there cannot get access to those exclusive deals and discounts you will only be providing for your fans; what it means is that to gain access, an outsider will have to first like your page in order to be granted the same privileged status as your already existing fans. Truly a great way to provide value for your existing fans as well as draw in more fans!

Tip 3 – Post at non-peak times

If you are posting at peak times using the *Insights* tool as we have already discussed but feel that you are not quite getting the engagement you want from your fans, then it might be a really good idea to post at non-peak times. This is the time when there is generally a lull in the traffic on Facebook and that is precisely what might get your post the visibility it deserves.

You could post during peak hours as well; just make sure you don't post too much as that will only flood the news feed of your fans' Facebook pages, and that is certainly not what they expected when they liked that Facebook page of yours in the first instance.

 # Tip 4 – Use Insights to track the engagement of your posts

As we have already seen, using Facebook Insights can be a great way to ensure that you post at just the right times and get the maximum engagement possible, but you should really be using it to its fullest to track the engagement of your posts over time.

We have already discussed the importance of having a sound tracking plan in the first chapter – this is how you do that very tracking. You will be able to see exactly how many likes, comments and shares each post has got and that will help you better craft your future posts. That way you will be going in the right direction and custom making posts for your fans based on exactly the type of material they want.

Tip 5 – Cross promote your page with others out there

Once you have reached a reasonable amount of likes, like say 1000, it will be a really good idea to cross promote that page out there with others that might be related to your industry or perhaps simply popular sites that have the same kinds of people that you are targeting, forming their fan base. All you have to do is ask them to promote your page with their target audience and in turn you will promote theirs as well.

Nobody is averse to free publicity and you will find that you can very easily gain a much larger number of fans with this very simple exercise. The more cross promotions you do out there, the better – just make sure you select only the best possible pages to do that promotion with!

Tip 6 – Create a call to action for your posts

Your posts might be pretty lucid, but are you even incorporating a call-to-action button along with them so that the people reading them can take some action that will truly benefit you? For instance, you might have posted a snippet about an online event you will be organizing soon; you have to ensure that you have a button alongside it that enables people to sign up for it.

If the call to action is not there, the *action* you seek from the end user will not come in all probability.

Tip 7 – Keep those posts short

The last thing you want is to keep those posts of yours far too long; make sure they are under 80 characters and see the difference in the kind of engagement levels you get!

 # Tip 8 – Tag your fans only if there is something very important you have to say

The last thing you want to do is keep tagging your fans in your posts. If there is something like the launch of a new product, do go ahead; otherwise it's best to respect their privacy or you might just lose a lot of precious fans in the process. If you keep tagging them it will only look like you are trying to get cheap publicity by making your business page known to all the friends of your fans.

On the other hand, when you are telling them something really important and tagging them every once in awhile they will know that you have done so only because you don't want them to miss out on that valuable piece of information you are trying to share with them.

 # Tip 9 - Make sure you always spell check that content

The last thing you want to do is to appear less than professional, and the easiest way to let that happen is by not proof checking your content before you post it out there. That will only make you look like an amateur. T

he audience is far more discerning than you might think and when you make even the slightest grammatical mistake, it has ramifications on your brand, the extent of which you will not be able to fathom. So, make sure you get that grammar right!

 # Tip 10 – Make sure you interact with your audience in a timely manner

We have already discussed the importance of interacting with your audience especially when you ask questions, but what you have to bear in mind is that you need to get back to their comments in not later than twenty-four hours. That potential customer of yours should know that you really care about him or her. Make sure you respond to each and every person on your site. You could even tag them in your comments so that you ensure they read what you have said in regards to their comment.

Conclusion

In this book we have seen all there is to know about the wonderful world of Facebook Marketing. We have seen exactly why Facebook marketing is ever so important in this digital world of ours and understood all the essentials that go into the making of a stellar Facebook marketing campaign.

We have also seen the top ten Facebook marketing strategies to get the most leverage out of that campaign of ours, as well as the best possible tips that we can use to make our brand shine even more brightly than we could have imagined, on the number one social media platform.

It's time then to take the plunge into the world of Facebook marketing and work towards capitulating your brand towards levels of success that you would have visualized only in your dreams.

All you have to do is ensure you take all the wonderful information contained in this book and set it into practice. In only a short period of time you will come to see that your brand is getting far more *likes* than you thought it would ever be capable of getting and your product, every ounce of the success and recognition it deserves.